A CREATIVE ARTS BIOGRAPHY

HANS CHRISTIAN ANDERSEN:
Immortal Storyteller

BY ELIZABETH RIDER MONTGOMERY
ILLUSTRATED BY RICHARD LEBENSON

ABOUT THE BOOK: The character of a sensitive man is treated with understanding in this biography of one of the world's greatest storytellers. The author brings Andersen to life for young readers as she integrates incidents from his personal life and writing career. This is a pilot book in Garrard's new series, *CREATIVE ARTS BIOGRA-PHIES*, which tell the life stories of the truly creative geniuses of the world. Providing hours of worthwhile pleasure reading, these books will help young people understand that success results not only from creative ability but also from hard work and a real determination to succeed.

Subject classification: Biography
Sub-classification: Authors, Reading

ABOUT THE AUTHOR: Elizabeth Rider Montgomery is a versatile author, having written fiction, nonfiction, textbooks, and plays. Most of her work is in the juvenile field, ranging from kindergarten through high school age. She has also contributed many articles and stories to children's magazines. Mrs. Montgomery's interests are as varied as her writing ability. She has written two of Garrard's *WORLD EXPLORER BOOKS*, a *DISCOVERY BOOK*, a *HOW THEY LIVED BOOK*, and an *INDIAN BOOK*. With good reason her *Hans Christian Andersen* was chosen as a pilot book in the firm's new *CREATIVE ARTS BIOGRAPHIES* series.

Reading Level: Grade 5   Interest Level: Grades 4–7
144 pages . . . 5¾ x 8¼   Publisher's Price: $2.49

Illustrated with photographs and line drawings; full-color jacket; reinforced binding; index; list of Andersen's most famous fairy tales

GARRARD PUBLISHING COMPANY

Hans Christian
ANDERSEN
IMMORTAL STORYTELLER

Hans Christian
ANDERSEN
IMMORTAL STORYTELLER

by Elizabeth Rider Montgomery

illustrated by Richard Lebenson

GARRARD PUBLISHING COMPANY

Champaign, Illinois

For Deborah Small

Photo Credits:

The Bettmann Archive: p. 16
The New-York Historical Society: p. 125
All other photos from the Royal Danish
    Ministry for Foreign Affairs, courtesy of
    the Danish Information Service, New York City.

Contents

60059

1. Hans Christian's Two Worlds

Once upon a time there was a little boy, and his name was Hans Christian Andersen. He lived in two worlds, the real world and a dream world.

In the real world Hans Christian was the son of a poor shoemaker and a washerwoman. They lived in the town of Odense, on the island of Fyn in Denmark. They lived in a one-room cobbler shop on a narrow cobblestone street.

In 1812 Hans Christian was seven years old. He was tall like his mother, Anne-Marie, and blond like his father, Hans.

One Monday morning Hans Christian looked at the toy theater his father had begun to make the day before.

"Please, Father," he begged, "won't you finish my theater before you mend those old shoes?"

The shoemaker liked to do what his little boy wanted. But today he shook his head.

"This is not Sunday," he answered. "I must work all day today. If I don't repair these shoes, we will have nothing to eat tomorrow."

The shoemaker began to work at his bench, and Anne-Marie started cleaning the room as she did every day. Hans Christian followed her around and sometimes helped. His mother swept the rough floor. She dusted the pictures on the wall and the chest of drawers that held their few extra clothes. A vase of flowers that Grandmother Andersen had brought stood on the chest. Grandmother came every day to visit, for she dearly loved her grandson. But Grandfather Andersen never came. His mind had failed years before, and Hans Christian was afraid of him.

Anne-Marie shook the feather quilts and made

The Andersen home in Odense, now a museum, is
visited by thousands of people every year.

up the beds. Hans Christian helped push his
folding crib under the big, curtained bed. Then
they went to the kitchen corner. Anne-Marie
washed the dishes and the tiled stove, and the
room was spotless.

As soon as the housework was finished,
Anne-Marie went down to the Odense River. She
washed clothes for other people. Winter and

summer she scrubbed clothes on flat stones in the river and beat them with a wooden paddle.

Hans Christian and his father were alone together. The boy sat on the floor beside his father's workbench. Outside, children played in the street, shouting and laughing. But Hans Christian did not go out to play with them. Other children teased him because he was tall and awkward. They thought he had queer ideas.

Usually the shoemaker talked to his son as he pounded and stitched his leather. Sometimes he took a book down from the shelf above his workbench. He would read aloud a story from the *Bible,* or from the *Arabian Nights,* or perhaps a play by Holberg, a Danish Writer.

Today, however, the shoemaker was too busy to read stories. Hans Christian had to amuse himself. He closed his eyes and went into his other world.

In his dream world, Hans Christian was not an ugly little boy whom other children mocked. He was not too tall and thin for his age, with long yellow hair and a great big nose. He did not have huge hands and enormous clumsy feet. He did not wear heavy wooden shoes and funny-looking outgrown clothes. He was not a poor shoemaker's son. And his mother did not have to wash clothes in the cold Odense River. Not at all!

In his dream world, Hans Christian Andersen was the handsome son of a powerful king. He lived in an elegant castle. He had beautiful clothes and delicious foods, with all the butter he wanted. Everybody knew him, and everybody loved him.

Most people would have laughed at the child's dreams. In Denmark at that time, poor people expected to remain poor all their lives. Poor children seldom became rich or famous. But the shoemaker did not believe this had to be so.

"You can do great things, my son, if you go to school," he said, while his hammer went *rat-a-tat-tat*. "Once you get an education, you can do anything you wish. If I had had more schooling, I would not have to make shoes for a living."

Hans Christian opened his pale blue eyes and came back to the real world. All he wanted was

This is a typical narrow, cobblestone street in Andersen's native town, Odense.

to be rich and famous. Surely it wasn't necessary to go to school for that!

There were no free schools at that time, and nobody had to attend school. A child of poor parents seldom got much education. Usually he was apprenticed at an early age. That is, he went to live with a carpenter, or a tailor, or a shoemaker, and there he learned to earn a living.

Hans Christian's parents, however, wanted their son to have a better life than theirs. So they had sent him to school, but he had stayed only a few days. The teacher punished him for not paying attention. The other children laughed at his dream-world stories.

"You are mad like your Grandfather Andersen!" they shouted.

The very thought of his weak-minded grandfather terrified Hans Christian. He had run home from school and refused to return.

His parents soon sent him to another school, but the boy would not study. All he did was draw pictures and make up stories. At last Anne-Marie decided school was a waste of money. After that she let Hans Christian stay at home.

Now, when his father started talking about school, Hans Christian did not want to listen. He went across the room and began to play with his toys.

The shoemaker had made many clever toys for his son. There were charming cut-out paper pictures. There was a little peep show. There were jumping jacks and other toys with moving parts. Hans Christian's favorite was a mill. When he pulled some strings, the mill worked and the miller danced. All afternoon the boy played with his toys. All afternoon his father worked on shoes. And his mother washed clothes in the Odense River.

In the evening Anne-Marie came home. She was tired and cold from standing knee-deep in the icy river for many hours. She made a thick soup for the family's supper. With it they ate dry black bread. There was seldom more than this to eat.

Soon after supper, Hans Christian had to go to bed. His folding crib crowded the small home-workshop, so he was allowed to lie in his parents' big bed until they needed it. Curtains hung all around the bed. It was like sleeping in a tent. The boy lay there dreaming, half-awake and half-asleep. When his father finished his toy theater, he thought, he would make up plays for it. What fun he would have with his new toy!

2. Bewitched by the Theater

"Tonight," announced the shoemaker, "we will go to the theater."

"The real theater?" asked Hans Christian. His eyes sparkled. He was almost too excited to eat his soup.

Several months had passed. The shoemaker had finished the toy theater and had made some puppets. Hans Christian spent hours playing with his puppet theater and making up plays for it. Tonight, however, would be his first visit to a real theater.

Anne-Marie washed and dressed her son for the occasion very carefully. She wanted everybody to admire him. She washed his long yellow hair and curled it. She pinned pieces of silk across his thin chest to look like a vest. Then she tied a big kerchief around his neck in a huge bow. And he was ready. Off they went through the cobblestone streets.

Hans Christian was truly enchanted with the theater. The play seemed very real to him.

An old engraving shows the square in Odense, Andersen's birth place.

When it was over, he said, "The theater is my favorite place. I would like to come here every night."

"The theater costs money," Anne-Marie reminded him as they walked home. "We must spend our money for food and clothes."

"The theater is a treat we can seldom afford," her husband agreed. "Perhaps some day, Hans Christian, I can take you to see another play. But it will not be soon."

"Some day" never came. Hans, the shoemaker, became a soldier and went away to war. He fought in the Danish army for Napoleon, the French Emperor who wanted to conquer Europe.

The French and Danish armies were beaten. Hans the soldier came home to Odense to be a shoemaker again. But he was sick and discouraged now. Napoleon was no longer the master of Europe. Denmark had lost not only the war, but also much of her land. For 400 years Norway had belonged to Denmark. Now Napoleon's victorious enemies gave Norway to

Sweden. Hans Andersen felt that his fighting had helped neither Napoleon, his idol; nor Denmark, his country. His life had been a complete failure. He prayed that his son would be more successful than he.

"No matter what the boy wants to be," he told his wife, "let him have his way, even if it is the silliest thing in the world."

When Hans Christian was eleven, the shoemaker died. The boy had loved his father dearly. Without him, the real world seemed almost unbearable. Hans Christian escaped from it into his dream world. While his mother washed clothes in the river, he played with his puppet theater. He made a tent out of a broomstick and his mother's apron under a gooseberry bush. There he played for hours at a time.

He had collected a ragbag of scraps of cloth and ribbon and lace. From these he made costumes for his puppets. It was amazing what neat stitches his big fingers could make!

Hans Christian longed to see a real play again, and he often hung around the theater.

The interior of Andersen's modest home.

Whenever a play came to Odense, Peter Juncker, an old soldier, distributed theater posters. This was a kind of advertising. The posters listed the actors and told about their play.

One day Peter Juncker noticed Hans Christian outside the theater. "If you will help me take these posters around," he said, "I will give you one."

The offer thrilled Hans Christian. Gladly he helped the old soldier deliver the posters. Then he took his poster home. He studied it carefully. He made up a play about the names on the poster, and presented it in his puppet theater.

After that, whenever a play came to Odense, Hans Christian helped distribute theater posters. Peter always gave him one to keep, and Hans Christian always made up a play about it.

Anne-Marie often worried about her son. He was growing fast. He was getting very, very tall and thin. Still he did no work nor did he study.

Several times Anne-Marie had tried to help Hans Christian prepare for the future. She had apprenticed him to a weaver, but he would not stay. A job in a tobacco factory did not last, either.

Again Anne-Marie put her son in school, but again it was a waste of money. Hans Christian learned to read. But he did not like spelling, arithmetic, history, or geography, and he would not study them.

"I am going to be an actor," he said grandly. "And actors do not need to bother with things like that."

Two years after his father died, Anne-Marie married again. The new stepfather took little interest in thirteen-year-old Hans Christian.

Sometimes the lonely boy went down to the river. He stood on a stone in his clumsy wooden shoes, and sang at the top of his voice. He sang all the songs he knew, and then he made up new ones.

An old washerwoman had told Hans Christian that China lay on the other side of the world. So the ignorant boy believed that the Emperor of China lived right underneath the Odense River. Some day, he thought, the Emperor would hear him sing. The Emperor would come up

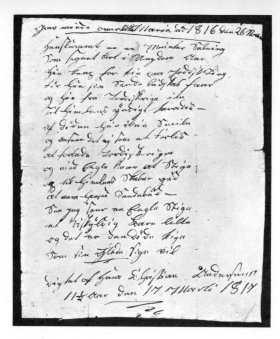

A poem written by Andersen as a child.

out of the river and greet him. Of course he would bring rich treasures with him.

The Emperor of China gave no sign that he heard Hans Christian singing. But neighbors heard his high sweet voice. Sometimes they asked him to come to their homes and sing for guests. Hans Christian was delighted. He dearly loved an audience. Usually he offered to recite as well. He repeated whole scenes from plays he had read or made up.

Often Hans Christian was given a few coins for

entertaining. It was wonderful to be given money for doing what he loved most to do! He took the coins home and dropped them in his clay pig bank.

One day a neighbor, Colonel Guldberg, took him to entertain Prince Christian, governor of the island.

"The Prince may ask what you want to do," the Colonel said. "If he does, say that you long to attend the Odense Grammar School."

This was the best school in town, but it was expensive. Anne-Marie could not afford to send her son there.

As they went inside the castle, Hans Christian looked around eagerly to see what a real castle looked like. The Prince greeted him kindly. Then Hans Christian began to sing and recite. When he stopped for breath, the Prince asked about his plans for the future.

"I promised to tell you," Hans Christian answered frankly, "that I long to go to the Odense Grammar School. But what I really want to do is to become an actor."

Prince Christian did not offer to send the boy to school. And he was not willing to help him become an actor. Instead he said rather coldly, "A poor boy like you should be apprenticed and learn a trade. I will help you become a carpenter, if you like."

Hans Christian thanked the Prince politely, but shook his head. Very disappointed, he left the castle. Why did everybody want him to go to school or learn a trade?

3. A Poor Boy Seeks His Fortune

Fourteen-year-old Hans Christian stood in the wings of the Odense theater. He was so excited that he could not stand still. In a few seconds he would go on stage. He would act in a play given by the Royal Theater of Copenhagen!

Hans Christian's friend, Peter Juncker, was responsible. When the actors came to town, the old soldier had persuaded them to let Hans Christian watch all the plays from backstage.

The boy had seemed so enchanted that the actors were amused. They adopted him as a mascot.

Tonight he had a part in *Cinderella*. He was a page, with two lines to speak. For hours he had been ready, dressed in his bright red costume.

Now it was time. Hans Christian walked out on the stage, spoke his two lines, and walked off happily. He was a real actor now!

"I shall go to Copenhagen," he told his mother grandly. "I shall be a member of the Royal Theater." Copenhagen was, and is, the capital of Denmark.

"What a foolish dream!" said Anne Marie. "We have no money for an actor's training." Actors had to have money to live on while they were learning.

"You are going to be a tailor," Anne-Marie went on sharply. "I will apprentice you to the tailor in the next street."

"No! No!" Hans Christian cried. "I could never be a tailor!"

"You will be a good tailor," Anne-Marie assured him. "See what clever costumes you make for your puppets. You are fourteen now. It is high time you learned a trade."

Hans Christian burst into tears. "Never!" he cried. "I shall be an actor, not a tailor!"

Anne-Marie had spoiled her son all his life. But for once she was stubborn. He would be a tailor, and that was that!

She repeated things she had heard: "Actors are starved to keep them thin. They have to drink oil to make their bodies bend easily. They are whipped often."

Anne-Marie really believed these foolish things. Maybe Hans Christian did too a little, but he did not care. Through his tears he said over and over, "I am going to be an actor. I am going to Copenhagen."

"How could you possibly go to Copenhagen?" his mother asked angrily. "You have no money for traveling, no money to live on when you get there."

Hans Christian ran to get his clay pig bank.

He smashed it with a rock and many coins tumbled out. He counted them eagerly.

"I have thirteen rix dollars!" he cried triumphantly. "That is a lot of money! I can certainly get to Copenhagen." He had no idea what it would cost to live in a big city, and neither had his mother.

Anne-Marie began to weaken. "What would you do in Copenhagen?" she asked uncertainly. "Who would take care of you?"

"I shall become famous," he replied confidently. "That's the way it goes, Mother. First one has to suffer terribly. Then one becomes famous."

He seemed so sure of himself that Anne-Marie gave up the tailor idea. Perhaps she remembered his father's words, "No matter what the boy wants to be, let him have his way, even if it is the silliest thing in the world."

"You ought to know somebody in Copenhagen before you go," she insisted. "It is a big, big city and you will need advice."

"I shall get a letter to Madame Schall," Hans

Christian told her. "She is the greatest dancer in the Royal Ballet. Mr. Iversen, who prints the theater posters, will write a letter for me. Then God will do the rest."

And off he ran to see the old printer.

Mr. Iversen listened to the boy's wild plan. Then he tried to talk him out of it.

"You have no idea how hard life will be, alone in a big city," the old man told him. "You should stay in Odense and learn a trade as your mother wishes."

"No, I cannot," Hans Christian replied quickly. "I must be a great actor."

The printer gave up at last. He had never met Madame Schall, but he wrote a letter to her.

"She won't help you," old Mr. Iversen warned. "Go to see Professor Rahbek instead. He is a director of the Royal Theater in Copenhagen."

Happy and excited, Hans Christian scarcely listened. He took the letter, thanked the old man, and dashed home.

Meanwhile his mother had consulted a fortune-teller. Her words comforted the superstitious

Anne-Marie: "Your son will have a better fortune than he deserves. He will be a wild bird flying high, admired by all the world. One day Odense will be decked with lights for him."

On September 3, 1819, Hans Christian was ready to leave Odense. His mother and grandmother saw him off on the mail coach. He was very proud of his new boots and a big top hat somebody had given him. He carried a small bundle of clothes, his puppet theater, and a little bread to eat on the long journey.

Hans Christian kissed his mother and his grandmother good-bye. All three of them wept. The coachman blew his horn and the mail coach started off. It rolled away from the gates of Odense, carrying Hans Christian Andersen out into the big world to seek his fortune. He was fourteen and a half, and he had ten rix dollars in his pocket. More important than the money, he had plenty of courage and complete faith in his future.

4. The Helpful Elves

Denmark is made up of many islands. Hans Christian took a coach across his own island of Fyn, then a ship to the island of Zealand. There he boarded another coach for the great city of Copenhagen, the capital of Denmark.

At last, after almost three days of traveling, the city came into view. Hans Christian was thrilled. The walled city looked like fairyland, with its pale green towers, fine palaces, and beautiful churches.

Copenhagen had four gates. They were locked at midnight and the keys were taken to the King. Hans Christian had been told that the King

slept with the keys of the city under his pillow.
This seemed reasonable to the innocent boy.

Hans Christian left his bundles at an inn. Then
he set out to find the Royal Theater.

Around and around the theater Hans Christian
walked. He was sure that in a short time he
would be a rich and famous actor there.

Early the next morning Hans Christian washed
carefully. He put on the suit his mother had
made for him out of an old suit of his father's.
It looked old-fashioned but he did not know it.
He put on his hat which was so big that it almost

The Royal Theater in Copenhagen.

covered his eyes. Then he went to call on the dancer, Madame Schall.

When he found the right building, Hans Christian hesitated before pulling the bell rope. He fell to his knees and prayed to God for help. Just as he finished his prayer, the door opened. A pretty servant girl came out, carrying a market basket. She smiled at the gawky boy kneeling on the steps and put a coin in his hand.

This bewildered Hans Christian. He was dressed in his new suit, good boots and a hat. It did nòt occur to him that anybody could mistake him for a beggar! He tried to return the coin, but the girl would not take it. She smiled again and went on to market.

It was very early. Hans Christian had to wait a long time before Madame Schall would see him.

The letter he brought puzzled the dancer. "I do not know this printer, Iversen," she said. "I can do nothing for you, boy."

Hans Christian smiled sweetly at the dancer and began to tell her the story of his life. The words tumbled over each other.

Then he showed how he could act. He recited scenes from plays. He took off his big boots and danced, holding his top hat like a tambourine. He did not understand why Madame Schall laughed. He had no idea how awkward he looked, with his long skinny legs and his immense clumsy feet. He thought she laughed because she enjoyed his dancing.

Suddenly Madame Schall stopped his performance and told him to leave. Hurt and bewildered, Hans Christian went outside. He sat on the doorstep with tears rolling down his cheeks.

Then he remembered what Mr. Iversen had said about Professor Rahbek, a director of the Royal Theater. As if by magic the tears stopped. Hans Christian's spirits rose swiftly. Surely Professor Rahbek would help him! The boy sprang to his feet and went to look for him.

Days later Hans Christian faced the truth. The Royal Theater of Copenhagen would not take him. Neither Professor Rahbek nor anybody else connected with the theater gave him any

encouragement. The money from his clay pig bank was almost gone. What was he going to do?

Through the streets of Copenhagen Hans Christian wandered. He circled the Royal Theater where he longed so much to act. He walked past the King's palace where the sentries in their bright blue and white uniforms stood guard. He was so hungry and discouraged, he scarcely knew where he went.

When he reached the harbor, he stared unseeingly at the sailing ships. One of those ships might be going to his home island of Fyn. Maybe the captain would take him.

"No!" thought Hans Christian. "Everybody will laugh at me if I go home a failure. It would be better to die."

For a few minutes the boy thought about different ways of dying. What would it be like to drown in the blue-green water of the harbor? Maybe freezing would be a more pleasant death. Winter would soon be here, and winters in Denmark were bitterly cold. Perhaps starving might be a better way to die, and it would be quick. He couldn't remember when he had last eaten.

Again Hans Christian went down on his knees. He prayed that God would protect him.

When he rose he had a happy idea. Maybe he could find somebody who would like his singing. Everybody in Odense thought he had a beautiful singing voice.

By four o'clock Hans Christian was standing on the steps of a voice teacher, Mr. Siboni. The housekeeper answered his ring.

"Mr. Siboni is entertaining at a dinner party," she said. "He cannot see anyone today."

Hans Christian's disappointment nearly choked him. "He must see me!" he protested. "If he doesn't, I shall have to go back to Odense. And I simply can't go back and let everybody know I'm a failure!"

Talking rapidly, almost wildly, Hans Christian told the housekeeper the story of his life. The good woman listened with increasing sympathy for the strange-looking overgrown child.

When Hans Christian stopped for breath, the

housekeeper told him to wait. She disappeared inside the house.

In a few minutes she was back. She had repeated his story to her master and his guests. They wanted him to come in and sing for them. Hans Christian could not have been happier if the skies had rained down gold pieces!

An hour later Hans Christian left the house, walking on air. Mr. Siboni and his guests had been very kind. Mr. Siboni promised to give him voice lessons. The guests had taken up a collection. Hans Christian would be given ten rix dollars every month to live on.

Hans Christian's dreams were coming true. Copenhagen was truly fairyland!

5. The Greedy Witch

For six months Mr. Siboni trained Hans Christian's voice. The boy slept at a cheap rooming house, and spent his days at Mr. Siboni's. He listened while the voice teacher taught other students. Sometimes he sat in the warm kitchen and talked to the kind housekeeper and the friendly cook. He had his fill of wholesome food. It was heaven!

Then one dreadful day he was turned out of heaven.

"Sing, Andersen," commanded Mr. Siboni. "Sing the scale."

Up the scale and down Hans Christian went. But when he reached the bottom of the scale, his voice broke. Instead of a deep note, a high, squeaky tone came out!

The boy's face grew red. This had happened several times lately. He seemed to have no control over his voice. He could never tell when it would be high and when it would be low. He had thought it was because his boots leaked and he often caught cold.

"So," said kind-hearted Mr. Siboni gently. "It is as I feared. Your voice is changing, Andersen. We can no longer continue the lessons. It is useless for you to return."

"Not return!" Hans Christian could not believe his ears. He had thought that this happy life would go on forever.

The teacher went on talking. "You must go back to your home, my boy. While your voice is changing we can do nothing with it. Besides, it is doubtful that you will ever be a singer."

"Then I shall become an actor," Hans Christian replied quickly. "I would really rather be an actor than a singer, anyway."

Mr. Siboni shook his head. "It is time you faced the truth, Andersen. The Royal Theater will never accept a boy with no education. It would be far better to go home and learn a trade like other poor boys."

"Never!" cried Hans Christian. He rushed from the house, sobbing as if his heart would break.

Again he wandered the streets of Copenhagen, discouraged, ragged, forlorn. How was he going to live?

He had made many friends in the six months he had been in Copenhagen. People could not

resist his sweet, loving nature. Most of his friends had helped him in one way or another. Still he could not bring himself to ask them for further help. And the money which Siboni's friends had collected for him was gone.

Going back to Odense was the sensible course, but Hans Christian did not consider it. He would think of some way to stay in Copenhagen. He had to!

Suddenly he remembered his childhood neighbor, the good, kind Colonel Guldberg. "He has a brother in Copenhagen!" Hans Christian cried aloud. "His brother will help me!" At once he set out to find him.

Professor Guldberg, a poet, turned out to be as kind as his brother, the Colonel. He offered to tutor the boy in Danish and German so that the Royal Theater might accept him some day. And he persuaded a friend to coach Hans Christian in acting.

Hans Christian had grown alarmingly during this half-year. He had kept his clothes clean and neat and mended, as he had been taught, but they were much too small now. Worse yet, his shoes were falling apart. Professor Guldberg gave him some new clothes and some cash. He also raised money for the boy among his friends.

Hans Christian's eyes filled with grateful tears when all these kindnesses were heaped on him. He thanked the poet over and over. Then he rushed back to his rooming house.

He had been renting a tiny cubbyhole of a room from a widow named Thorgesen. It was an empty pantry without any windows. There was just room in it for a bed, nothing else. The only air came through a couple of holes in the wall from the adjoining kitchen. Now, however, he could find a decent place to live.

"Such luck!" he told Mrs. Thorgesen. "I have found the most wonderful friend!" And he told her how kind and generous Professor Guldberg had been. His passion for story-telling made him exaggerate.

The widow Thorgesen's eyes began to gleam with greed. During the months that Hans Christian had lived in her house, she had learned how innocent he was. She made up her mind to get that money for herself.

"Come into my parlor," said Mrs. Thorgesen, taking Hans Christian's arm and pulling him along. "I am fond of you, and I am going to be very generous and kind."

Hans Christian was always ready to believe that people were good. He smiled his sweet, trusting smile. "You are very kind, I'm sure," he answered.

"Besides your room I am going to give you meals," said the landlady.

"I had thought of getting a larger room," the boy replied.

"Why do you need a larger room?" the widow demanded. "You have a bed. That is all you need. You may sit in my kitchen whenever you like and have your meals there. All this will cost only 20 rix dollars a month! Did you ever hear of anything so generous?"

"Twenty rix dollars!" gasped Hans Christian. "I couldn't possibly pay that much. Sixteen rix dollars a month is all I will have."

"Twenty rix dollars," the landlady repeated firmly. "Room and board."

Hans Christian shook his head. He tried to leave the parlor, but the widow clutched his arm.

"You won't dare leave here!" she snapped. "If you go, there is no telling what will happen to you. Copenhagen is a wicked, wicked city. Evil people lie in wait for innocent boys from the country. There are thieves, murderers, cheats, indecent people. You'll be in frightful danger if you leave my house. But here you will be safe."

Fifteen-year-old Hans Christian began to shiver with fear. Soon he felt that he would never dare live any place else. He begged Mrs. Thorgesen to let him stay.

"I will pay you fourteen rix dollars," he promised. "Please let me stay!"

The widow refused. "Not a cent less than 20. That is little enough to pay for room and board, and protection from the villains lurking in this evil city."

' Hans Christian began to weep. "But I can't pay that much!"

"You must," the greedy woman insisted. "I will give you time to think it over." She went out and locked the parlor door.

Poor Hans Christian! Only a little while ago he had come from Professor Guldberg's house, wild with happiness. He had been certain that everything was going to be all right. Now he was sinking in a sea of despair.

Suddenly the door opened. The widow came back in.

"I have decided," she announced, "to let you stay for only sixteen rix dollars a month."

To innocent Hans Christian this was a miracle! He fell to his knees and thanked God. Then he kissed the hand of the greedy landlady. He did not understand that she had decided he was telling the truth when he said sixteen rix dollars was all he would have. She would take what she could get and stop trying to squeeze more out of him.

"You are so good to me!" the boy cried.

Only later did Hans Christian realize what he was doing. He was giving up all the money that Professor Guldberg had promised him! He would not have a cent left for clothes, or boots, or books! But at least he would be safe from thieves and cheats and cut-throats.

6. "First One Has To Suffer"

The landlady's promise to let Hans Christian sit in her kitchen was worthless. Nearly every evening she entertained a gentleman caller there, and Hans Christian felt in the way. He preferred to take his supper to his room on a tray. There he sat in bed and ate. Then he read, by candlelight, stories and plays which a librarian friend lent him.

Often Hans Christian played with his puppet theater, or made costumes. Whenever he passed a tailor shop or a hat shop, he stopped in. The

shopkeepers often gave him scraps of ribbon or lace or silk for puppet clothes. When he could find paper to write on, he scribbled plays for his little theater.

Whenever he was allowed to, he watched the plays put on in the Royal Theater from the wings. Sometimes he even had a free seat in the balcony. This was heaven!

In the daytime Hans Christian divided his time among his lessons. He studied acting with Professor Guldberg's friend, Latin with another friend, and Danish and German with the Professor himself. He studied dancing with Mr. Dahlén, a ballet dancer who had a school.

Mr. Dahlén did not believe that the homely boy with the clown-like figure could ever be a dancer. Still he became a good friend to Hans Christian. Often he took the boy home with him for dinner. The Dahlén children loved to see him come.

"Here is Hans Christian!" they would cry. "Tell us a story, Hans Christian. Tell us a story."

They would settle down around him and he would begin. "Once upon a time. . . ."

The story might be one his father had read to him, or one his grandmother's friends had told him, or one he made up himself. Always it was told vividly, with gestures. The children were enchanted. It was like watching a play in the theater!

Sometimes Hans Christian brought his puppet theater to the Dahlén home and put on plays. Sometimes he made delicate cut-out pictures, as his father had done for him. He made storks standing on one leg, windmills, chimney sweeps, fairies. He also made up games for the children. The entire family became very fond of the serious gawky boy with the long yellow hair.

Months passed in this way. Soon more than a year had gone by. At last Mr. Dahlén had to tell Hans Christian that the dancing lessons must stop. He would never be a dancer. There was no use wasting more time.

Hans Christian's acting lessons came to an end, too. The teacher said he would never become an actor. The lessons in Danish, German, and Latin had long since ended, for the boy would not study. He had often skipped his lessons. Professor Guldberg became very angry with him. All Hans Christian cared about was the theater. Lessons in languages seemed unimportant.

Only one contact with the theater was left to Hans Christian now. The Royal Theater allowed him to act as an extra occasionally, without pay. Whenever a play called for a crowd scene, he went on stage with many others. He hunched over to keep his outgrown jacket and pants from parting company. He tugged at his sleeves, trying to pull them down to his bony wrists. He shuffled his feet along the floor so the holes in his shoes would not show. But at least he was acting!

The year of 1821 drew to a close. Hans Christian was almost seventeen.

On New Year's Day he said to himself, "I shall go to the Royal Theater today." Someone had told him an old superstition: Whatever one did on New Year's Day, one would do throughout the coming year. Hans Christian was as superstitious as his mother, and he believed it.

"I shall stand on the stage," he decided, "and

Andersen's fanciful imagination is shown in one
of his paper cut-out pictures.

recite every single play I know. Then I will be certain to be a real actor all year long!"

The Royal Theater was closed for the holiday. A half-blind doorkeeper napped at the stage entrance. Hans Christian slipped past without being discovered, and tiptoed out on the empty stage.

How dark and frightening the big auditorium was! How icy and scary the bare stage looked! As Hans Christian stood there, he forgot every play he had ever learned. He could not recall a single scene, not even a line!

Hans Christian fell to his knees and began to recite the Lord's Prayer aloud. When he finished, he uttered a heartfelt prayer of his own.

"It will be better with me soon," he ended. "Won't it, God?"

He scrambled to his feet, comforted, and stole away past the snoozing doorman. Outside the theater, he drew a deep breath. This year was sure to bring him success!

7. Enter the Fairy Godfather

In the succeeding months, however, there was no sign of success. Hans Christian never knew how he got through that long cold winter of 1822.

He moved at last from greedy Mrs. Thorgesen's house into a cheaper but bigger room. He was supposed to eat his meals out, but his kind-hearted new landlady gave him a cup of coffee for breakfast. This, and a roll of bread, was often all he had to eat the whole day long. All winter he was on the verge of starvation. The only real meals he ever had were in the homes of friends.

The only clothes he had were those that friends gave him. Since he was taller and thinner than anyone else, these clothes never fitted. They made him look thinner and more awkward than he really was. However, they kept him from freezing.

Somebody gave him a good blue coat, but it was far too big across the chest for skinny Hans Christian. Once, when he was invited to a party, he stuffed the front of the coat with old theater programs to make it fit better. At the party people urged him to take off his coat, but Hans Christian would not. He left long before the party ended, rather than show what he had done.

Nearly all his life Hans Christian had been making up plays for his puppet theater. Now he began to write plays for the real theater.

"If the Royal Theater will not have me as actor, dancer, or singer," he said, "they will produce the plays I write." Thus Hans Christian Andersen went into the field that was to bring him fame — writing.

His first play was based on a German story.

He called it *The Chapel in the Forest*. To his great disappointment, Professor Guldberg forbade him to submit it to the Royal Theater.

Although his fingers were so cold he could scarcely hold a pen, Hans Christian wrote another play secretly. This was *The Robbers of Vissenberg*, based on a popular legend. The handwriting was messy and the spelling fantastically bad. Nevertheless Hans Christian sent it to the Royal Theater. He had made a beginning in his career.

After six weeks, *The Robbers of Vissenberg* was returned with a letter.

"The young man should seek an education," said the letter, "or the career he is so eager to adopt must be forever closed to him." The letter was signed with four names. The fourth name was Jonas Collin, Councillor to the King.

Hans Christian stared at the letter unseeingly. Education — study — school! How often during his life had he heard those words! He remembered his father telling him he could do anything he wanted, once he got an education. He remem-

bered Colonel Guldberg advising him to ask Prince Christian to send him to school. Later the Colonel's brother, Professor Guldberg, had urged him to study his language lessons. Many friends also had told him that he needed an education.

Now at last, at the age of seventeen, Hans Christian began to believe it.

But how could he go to school? Education in Denmark was not free, and he had no money. He did not even have money for food and clothes. Unless he could sell a play he had no money for anything!

To complete his despair, in May he received a notice from the Royal Theater. His services as an extra at the theater were no longer needed. Now he had no connection whatever with his beloved theater. His two-and-a-half years in Copenhagen had brought him nothing but failure!

Desperately Hans Christian began to write another play. He scribbled away at top speed. In two weeks he had completed *The Elves' Sun.*

Each play he wrote Hans Christian read to anyone who would listen. He simply had to have

Rear Admiral Peter Frederik Wulff

an audience. Early one morning, therefore, Hans Christian took the manuscript of *The Elves' Sun* and went to call on a perfect stranger, Admiral Wulff.

"You have translated Shakespeare," the boy said as soon as the admiral had greeted him. "I love his work too. I have also written a play and if you'll only listen. . . ."

Admiral Wulff had no chance to refuse. Hans Christian began to read his play aloud while his host was showing him to a chair.

Andersen spent many happy hours in the magnificent Wulff family home.

When he had finished reading, Hans Christian asked, "Do you think I shall amount to anything? I wish it so much."

The kind-hearted admiral did not like to tell the strange boy that his play had completely confused him. Instead he invited him to come back again some day.

"Thank you, I will," Hans Christian answered gladly. "I'll come back when I have written a new play. That will be in about two weeks."

Hans Christian submitted *The Elves' Sun* to the Royal Theater. Then he began to write another play. When he had finished it he went back to Admiral Wulff's house. This time he met the rest of the family. The one he liked best was the little hunchbacked daughter, Henriette, who was only a year older than he. She had a clever mind and a gay, sparkling disposition. The oddly assorted pair — the overgrown gangling boy and the tiny cripple — became firm friends.

Mrs. Wulff was as kind as her husband and she too liked Hans Christian. But she did not hesitate to tell him that his plays could never be successfully produced.

Henriette Wulff

"They might be made into good stories," Mrs. Wulff told the young author, "but they aren't really plays. They couldn't possibly be staged."

Some people, like the admiral, listened politely to Hans Christian's plays. Some listened sympathetically, like Henriette, and some even praised his work. A few, like Mrs. Wulff, told him frankly that his plays would never be accepted for the stage.

Hans Christian loved praise. It was as necessary to him as sunshine is to a plant. But criticism crushed him. Usually it made him burst into tears.

Every morning that summer Hans Christian woke up hoping that today he would hear from the Royal Theater that his play had been accepted. Every night he went to bed heavy-hearted as well as hungry.

At last, in September, Hans Christian received a summons to appear before the directors of the Royal Theater. Wild with happiness, he washed and dressed carefully. Quivering with excitement, he presented himself for the interview.

Professor Rahbek spoke first. This was the man Hans Christian had called on when he first came to Copenhagen.

"Here is your play, *The Elves' Sun*," said Professor Rahbek, handing it to him. "Your so-called play is nothing but a string of words, Andersen. There is no dramatic action, no plan, and no real characters. In short, the play is entirely unsuitable for the stage."

Hans Christian's heart thudded into his boots. Trembling with deep disappointment, he waited silently. They were going to tell him to stop bothering them with his plays. They would tell him to go back to Odense and learn a trade.

Then Jonas Collin, Councillor to the King of Denmark, began to speak. He said something very different from what Hans Christian had expected to hear.

"Your play shows that you have some ability, Andersen," he said. "If you are willing to study, you might write a good play some day."

Councillor Collin's quiet words touched the boy deeply. Tears came to his eyes.

Mr. Collin went on to say, "The directors have decided to send you to school. I myself shall speak to the King about a scholarship grant."

Hans Christian did not know that Denmark had a fund for artists and writers. Promising artists were given money to live on or to pay for their studies. First, however, the King must approve their names.

With a full heart, Hans Christian thanked the directors of the Royal Theater, especially Jonas Collin. He felt as if Councillor Collin were his fairy godfather!

8. The Cruel Ogre

It was Monday morning, October 28, 1822. Hans Christian was ready to enroll in the grammar school at Slagelse, about 50 miles from Copenhagen.

He looked neat. He had new clothes from head to foot—clothes that actually fitted him! The boots had been made for him. Tall and lanky he still was, and would always be. He had extremely long arms and legs and huge feet. Now that he was properly dressed, however, he didn't look like a scarecrow any more.

Hans Christian felt as if he had rubbed Aladdin's lamp, and the genie had granted his wishes. But really God had done it — God and Jonas Collin. The kind State Councillor had persuaded the King of Denmark that Hans Christian Andersen should have 350 rix dollars a year! Now he could have proper clothes, food, books, everything he needed! Hans Christian breathed a prayer of thanks to God, and added a sincere postscript for Jonas Collin.

Rector Simon Meisling was headmaster of the Slagelse Grammar School. He looked up as ugly, skinny Hans Christian entered his office. Behind his thick glasses, the Rector's little eyes glittered. He was very jealous of this boy because he wanted a royal grant himself. He wanted to write poetry instead of teaching. But the King did not offer him any money!

"Your name?" he snapped.

"Hans Christian Andersen."

"Your age?"

"Seventeen and a half."

Rector Meisling snorted. "You should be in

college by now, instead of a grammar school, a great galoot like you! You must be an idiot!"

Hans Christian started to explain, but the headmaster cut him short. "I'm not interested in alibis," he snarled. "Let us see how much you know, so we can tell which class to put you in. How much Latin have you studied?"

Trembling with fear, Hans Christian tried to think. What had he learned in those few Latin lessons Professor Guldberg's friend had given him?

"Tell me what this means," Rector Meisling commanded. He repeated a Latin sentence. Hans Christian stared blankly.

"No Latin," snapped the headmaster, making a black mark on the boy's record. "Any Greek?"

Dumbly Hans Christian shook his head.

"How far did you get in history?" Meisling asked. "Ancient? Middle Ages? Modern?"

Still Hans Christian stared. He did not know what the Rector was talking about. Besides, he could hardly take his eyes off of the man's dirty clothes and messy red hair. His mother had taught him to be clean and neat, no matter how poor he was. He could not understand Rector Meisling — going to school with gravy on his vest, egg on his shirt-front, and dirt under his fingernails.

The headmaster's voice grew still colder and sharper as he questioned his new student. Geography? The boy knew nothing of it. He couldn't even find Copenhagen on the map!

Arithmetic? Hans Christian knew a little about addition and subtraction. Nothing else whatever.

His handwriting was terrible. He couldn't spell the simplest words. He could read, to be sure, but all he had ever read were plays or novels. Nothing worthwhile at all!

At the end of an hour, the untidy headmaster led the neat new student out of his office. Hans Christian towered over the short, stubby Rector. They walked into the second grade classroom.

Many little boys were seated at long benches. They were half Hans Christian's height, and less than half his age.

"Here is a new classmate for you," Rector

Meisling told the small boys. "Here is a great big dunce who hasn't yet learned to write and to figure properly. I hope you little fellows will show him how proper Danish boys study."

Hans Christian's face grew red. He wanted to sink through the floor. It was all he could do to keep from crying.

At a signal from the second-grade teacher, he tried to fit his long legs under a bench. Everybody laughed to see how he had to bend them almost double. The headmaster laughed loudest of all.

Thus began the long nightmare of Hans Christian's school years. Each day he spent hour after hour on his studies, and worked far into the night. Yet he was teased and humiliated in class.

The Rector encouraged the students to laugh at Hans Christian. When a herd of cattle passed the school building, he would order a class, "Stand up, boys, and look out the window. See Andersen's brothers passing by!"

If Hans Christian began to cry, Meisling would

say to a small boy, "Go and get a brick for Andersen to wipe his eyes on. The tears of the great poet Andersen will make even a brick poetical!"

Often the cruel headmaster called the boy "Shakespeare with the vampire eyes."

"Did you ever see anyone as ugly and stupid?" he would ask the class. Poor Hans Christian never learned to take these taunts without weeping.

The boy wrote to Jonas Collin about his troubles in school, but the Councillor thought he exaggerated.

"You must ignore the laughter and the teasing, Andersen," Collin wrote back. "Study hard and you will be promoted. Soon you will be with students your own age. Then you will no longer feel humiliated."

Councillor Collin was partly right. As Hans Christian worked and studied, he was promoted. Most of his teachers and fellow students came to respect him and like him. But the headmaster never changed his attitude. He continued to take out his jealousy and unhappiness on the unlucky boy. Mrs. Meisling treated him cruelly too.

During these dark, dark days, Hans Christian couldn't even comfort himself with his puppet theater, as he had done all his life. He had no time whatever for play or recreation. And Jonas Collin had advised him not to do any writing except school work. Life was hard indeed!

Jonas Collin

9. Good and Evil Magic

The only thing that made these school years
bearable was an occasional vacation. Then Hans
Christian was allowed to go to Copenhagen and
visit his friends.

Some of his happiest hours were spent in
Admiral Wulff's home. Henriette's merry nature
raised his spirits, and helped him to make light
of his troubles. She sympathized with him. She
also tried to teach him to laugh at difficulties.

Often Hans Christian visited in the home of
Jonas Collin. The Councillor was very pleased

with the progress he was making in school. The Councillor told his family to welcome the boy and to make him one of them.

The five Collin children tried to obey, but they found it hard to accept someone who was so unlike themselves. They were all calm, sensible, and practical, while Hans Christian was very flighty, moody, and impractical. His spirits swooped from the heights of joy to the depths of despair. A friendly word made him wildly happy, and a harsh word made him wretched all day long. And what an extravagant imagination he had!

Besides, Hans Christian looked so funny. He was an ugly, awkward bean pole of a boy with a long, oldish face, bulging nose, pale eyes and pale hair. He wore a pair of yellow cotton trousers which reached only halfway down his stick-like legs.

Hans Christian, on the other hand, took the entire Collin family to his heart at once. He loved them as if they were his very own family. He adored the youngest daughter, Louise, and

Louise Collin

he told her stories and made up games for her. He enjoyed talking and joking with the witty, oldest daughter, Ingeborg. And sober, steady Edvard, who was a little younger than he, came to mean more to Hans Christian than any other friend.

For Jonas Collin himself, the boy felt a deep affection and boundless gratitude. All of his life Hans Christian spoke of the Councillor as "the father."

As good as the Collins were to him, however, Hans Christian realized that they did not care as much for him as he did for them. They continually tried to make him over, to make him like themselves. They scolded and lectured him. They poked good-natured fun at him. Only Louise was gentle and patient and truly sympathetic. Only Louise never scolded or teased him. But like the others, Louise did not really believe that he would be famous some day.

One vacation Hans Christian went back to Odense for a visit. It was like a happy dream.

On the very first street he met his mother. He had grown so much and changed so greatly that she didn't recognize him at first. When she realized at last who he was, she was beside herself with joy. She stood him off and looked at him, as if she could never get enough of seeing him.

She took him around to all of her friends and acquaintances. She wanted them to see what a fine man her son had turned out to be. The grocer, the bookseller, clerks, washerwomen — all had to be shown. She was very, very proud of him. The only cloud on the visit was Hans Christian's sorrow about his grandmother. She had died recently.

Each time that Hans Christian returned to school after a vacation, life under Simon Meisling seemed worse than ever. The Rector knew that the boy was very sensitive about the matter of his future success. So he took to mocking Hans Christian almost daily.

"You're a stupid yokel who will never amount to anything!" the headmaster would shout in front of the whole school. "All the money that Denmark is spending on you is wasted, completely wasted!"

Each time Hans Christian heard this it hurt him unbearably. It wasn't true, he told himself. It simply couldn't be true. But he could never help wondering—what if Meisling were right?

As time went on, Simon Meisling treated Hans Christian worse and worse. He made the boy move into his home to live. For the first time in his life, Hans Christian had to live in dirty, messy surroundings.

Wicked Simon Meisling haunted Andersen for the
rest of his life.

Meisling gave him scanty helpings of food,
and only allowed him five small pieces of wood
for his fire, even in the coldest weather. He
made Hans Christian take care of his children
after school hours, locking them in the house
together.

The poor boy had little time for studying, and
he had no free time whatever now. As the
months passed, the Meislings gave him less and
less to eat, and insulted him more and more.
Sometimes Hans Christian became so depressed
and discouraged with his miserable life that he
was tempted to kill himself.

Years later Hans Christian Andersen wrote about his suffering:

"The life I led during these days still comes back to me in bad dreams. Once again I sit in a fever on the school bench. I cannot answer, I dare not, the angry eyes stare at me, laughter and gibes echo around me. These were hard and bitter times. . . . I almost broke under treatment which became ever crueller, all too cruel to be borne. Each morning I prayed to God that I should be spared the day to come! In the school the Rector took pleasure in mocking me, making fun of my person, and discussing my lack of talent. And when school was over, I found myself in his house."

At last Hans Christian felt he could not endure any more. Just in time somebody reported to Jonas Collin how the boy was treated by the

Meislings. The Councillor sent for Hans Christian. He was to return to Copenhagen at once.

When he said good-bye to the Rector, Hans Christian tried hard to be polite.

"Thank you for all the good you have done me," he said.

The headmaster was furious because Councillor Collin had found out about his behavior. He shrieked at Hans Christian, "You will never become a writer! Your verses will rot in a bookseller's attic, and you will end your days in a madhouse!"

Hans Christian ran from the house, sobbing. The four-and-a-half-year nightmare was over. But for the rest of his life, it would continue to haunt his dreams.

10. Still Bewitched by the Theater

The next two years were busy and happy ones for Hans Christian. Jonas Collin rented a little room for him and hired a tutor. Every day Hans Christian walked across Copenhagen from his attic room to his tutor's house. On the way over in the morning, his mind was on his studies. But on the return trip, his mind was free to wander far and wide. His eyes and ears and nose took in everything along the way.

Hans Christian started dropping in at the Collin home almost every day. Sometimes Mrs. Collin would invite him to stay for dinner. Often Edvard helped him with his Latin. He got sisterly lectures from Ingeborg and sober, sensible advice from Edvard and his father. Louise listened sympathetically to his little troubles. The Collins became dearer and dearer to him.

As soon as he passed his university examinations, Hans Christian wrote a book about his daily walks. He called it *A Journey on Foot from Holmen's Canal to the Eastern Point of Amager.* It was a lighthearted collection of thoughts, impressions, and emotions. Literary critics had little praise for it because the style was not dignified and serious. But readers enjoyed its gay humor and its vivid descriptions of Copenhagen. Hans Christian was delighted when people told him they had read his book and liked it.

Then on April 25, 1829, he had an even greater thrill. One of his plays was produced by the Royal Theater!

Hans Christian stood in the wings of the theater and waited for the first performance to begin.

Seven years had passed since he had repeated the Lord's Prayer on that stage. Then he had been penniless, homeless, hungry. Today he was a respected student, an author, and a dramatist. How good God had been to him!

The 24-year-old author looked almost distinguished now. Years of patient endurance under Meisling's cruel torments had given him quiet dignity. He would never lose his lovable childlike qualities of wonder and hope and trustfulness, but he was a man at last.

The play began. As he watched, Hans Christian could hardly bear the suspense. Would the audience like *Love on Saint Nicholas Church Tower?* Or would they hiss it?

The curtain fell on the final scene. From the other side of the curtain came a storm of applause.

"Bravo!" cried the audience. "Bravo! Bravo!"

Hans Christian could scarcely breathe for relief and joy. The audience liked it! His play was a success! He had taken a big step toward his goal.

Then another shout arose from the audience. "Author! Author! Long live Andersen!"

The actors tried to push Hans Christian out onto the stage for a curtain call. But he held back, suddenly terrified. He would burst into tears, he knew, if he faced the audience. Then they would laugh instead of applaud. He broke away from the friendly hands and ran from the theater as if goblins were after him.

Hans Christian did not stop running until he reached the home of Jonas Collin. Then he dropped into a chair and sobbed loudly.

Mrs. Collin was the only member of the family at home. She heard his sobs. She thought his play had failed, and she came in to comfort him.

"Hush, hush," she said soothingly, stroking his fair hair. "It's not the end of the world, my boy. Many a great playwright was not successful at first. Many a writer had his plays hissed off the stage."

Hans Christian sobbed louder than ever. "But they didn't hiss!" he cried. "They clapped! They cried, 'Bravo!' They shouted, 'Long live Andersen!'"

Mrs. Collin was astounded. She did not understand this strange, sensitive young fellow. Hans Christian had been in their home almost daily for the past two years, and she looked on him as another son by now. Nevertheless, she would never really understand him. He was just too different from her own normal, level-headed children.

Now that he was a real dramatist, Hans Christian was given a free pass to performances at the Royal Theater. How delighted he was!

As a successful author, he also began to be invited to the elegant homes of wealthy people. That summer of 1829 he went for a long visit at the country estate of Chamberlain Bang. What a wonderful time he had! There were picnics and garden parties, singing and games. Hans Christian enjoyed everything, and he liked everybody.

And how the children of the Bang family loved him! Hans Christian was always ready to entertain them, as he used to entertain the Dahlén children. He no longer had his puppet theater, but he had not forgotten how to make charming cut-out pictures and make up games. Besides, he could tell marvelous stories. Any time Hans Christian sat down, he was likely to be surrounded by children.

"Tell us a story," they would beg. "Please, Hans Christian, tell us a story."

Hans Christian would smile his kind, affection-

ate smile and he would begin, "Once upon a time, there was a prince. . . ."

The children would listen, enchanted. The grownups in the background would listen, too, almost as interested as the children themselves.

When the story ended, the grownups would look at each other and smile. Somebody was sure to say, "What a charming story! This Andersen is a clever fellow. He really ought to write down those stories some day."

11. The Stork

Six years went by, however, before Hans Christian Andersen began to write down any of his fairy tales.

In the fall of 1829, he passed his final university examinations. Now he had more time for writing, and he wrote as fast as he could. He wrote poems, plays, opera stories, one after another.

He also wrote travel books, for he had begun to travel. He traveled around Denmark. He went to Germany, to Switzerland, to France, to Sweden, and to Italy.

A sketch of Rome by Andersen.

For the first time in his life, he saw great mountains, sun-bathed lands, warm lakes, lemon trees and orange trees. He saw cathedrals, many fine paintings and sculptures, and famous buildings. Most of all, he saw people, rich and poor, great and small. He saw people of all kinds and descriptions.

Wherever Hans Christian went, he described

everything in his diary. He also made sketches to help him remember things. There were no real cameras at that time, so his sketches took the place of the photographs that travelers take today.

"I am becoming good at drawing," he wrote to Edvard Collin on one of his first journeys. "The artists in Rome all praise my sharp eye. In any case all my sketches (already over a hundred) are a treasure to me and will give me pleasure at home."

Later on Hans Christian went to Greece, Turkey, Spain, and England. He became the most traveled man in Denmark. His battered traveling bag and his hatbox became familiar sights all around Europe. So did his tall hat and his umbrella.

In his earlier journeys Hans Christian traveled by public coaches, for there were no railroads yet outside of England. When at last he had the chance to ride in a train, he was wildly excited. After that the railroad was his favorite means of travel.

"It is like flying!" he said. "I know now how the birds of passage feel. Just think, we covered 70 miles in three hours!"

Birds of passage, that migrated every year, had always fascinated Hans Christian. He often spoke of himself as a stork, Denmark's favorite bird. He even looked like a stork, with his pipe-stem legs and his long neck! Now that he was becoming successful, he could smile at himself. But he still could not bear to have

Andersen's traveling bags are preserved in his house in Odense. He always took a strong rope with him in case of fire.

others laugh at him. In a story he wrote later called *The Storks,* the young storks cannot bear to be teased either.

From early childhood Hans Christian had loved to watch the storks. Denmark is so far north that the winters are long and cold, with very short days and very long nights. The storks go south every year to escape the freezing Danish winter. In the fall, Hans Christian would watch them flying around in great circles. All at once they would take off on their journey to the warm countries.

"They must get a tingling in their wings," he thought. "Then they know it is time to fly south."

Hans Christian, too, sometimes felt a tingling, and he knew he must take another trip.

In the spring, the storks returned to Denmark. Year after year they came back to the very same nests on their favorite rooftops. It was considered lucky to have storks nesting on one's roof.

Hans Christian, too, had a favorite house to which he always returned. This was the Collin

The residence of Jonas Collin in Bredgade was
Andersen's favorite "home away from home." An
old engraving shows him with Collin's family.

home. Both his mother and his grandmother
were dead now, and he had no relatives at all.
He never married.

Jonas Collin and his family meant more to
Hans Christian than any other friends, even
Henriette Wulff. Their affection was precious,
and their opinion more important than that of
anyone else.

Even after all these years, Hans Christian did
not feel that the Collin family fully accepted him.

They still looked on him as a rather queer adopted brother. When Louise, the youngest girl, grew up, he fell in love with her. The Collin family did not approve of him as a husband for Louise, but not a word was said to him about it. They simply announced her engagement to another man without giving him any warning.

"No matter how good people are to me," Hans Christian said sadly to Edvard, "I continue to be an outsider."

Edvard, too, hurt him deeply. Hans Christian considered Edvard his very best friend. Yet Edvard would not allow him to use the Danish word for "you" that meant they were equals! Would the Collin family, Hans Christian wondered wistfully, ever really return his regard for them?

After five years of writing and traveling, Hans Christian wrote a novel, called *The Improvisator*. This was the story of an Italian poet who continually made up verses and stories. It really was the story of Hans Christian himself. Several characters in the book were real people who had helped him, or who had tried to hinder him.

The novel pictured Italy and its people, but it also showed the trials and sufferings that a poet had to endure. Into *The Improvisator* Hans Christian poured his experiences and his feelings. He expressed his deep need as a poet for appreciation and praise, and the harmful effect of criticism.

When he finished the novel, Hans Christian dedicated it to the Collins:

"To Councillor Collin and his noble wife, in whom I found parents, and to his children, in whom I found brothers and sisters—I bring the best I possess to the home of homes."

Hans Christian gave the finished manuscript to Edvard Collin, who had begun to act as his business agent. Edvard would try to find a publisher for the book.

"I don't care when the book is published," he told Edvard, "but I must have money now!"

Thus far his published writings had brought

Edvard and Henriette Collin

him little money. And his travels had used up his grant from the king. He did not even have enough left to pay next month's rent on his cheap attic room! He had worked for months on his novel, but he could not rest, even though it was finished. Edvard tried to get some money in advance from a publisher for *The Improvisator*.

Andersen's famous story of *The Princess and the Pea* inspired this statue by Georg Lober.

Meantime, Hans Christian set to work on a two-act opera, *Little Christine*. The Royal Theater promptly accepted it for production, but still he needed cash!

Suddenly Hans Christian had an idea. Perhaps he could sell some of his fairy tales. He might get enough money to keep him going for a while.

Hans Christian thought over the stories he had told through the years. He decided to write the story of the soldier and the tinder box first. This was a Danish folk tale, much like his favorite story, *Aladdin and His Wonderful Lamp*. Hans Christian had told *The Tinder Box* so often that he had worked out his own personal style.

Andersen dipped his quill pen into the ink. In his small, spiky handwriting he began to write:

> "There came a soldier marching down the high road — *one, two! one, two!* He had his knapsack on his back and his sword at his side as he came home from the wars. On the road he met a witch. . . ."

In Denmark at that time, authors were expected to write in a dignified literary style. But Hans Christian Andersen would not. He wrote exactly as he talked, in the very words he used when he told the story to children. Quite likely he told the story aloud to himself as he wrote. He needed to hear how the words sounded, so that he could avoid bookish-sounding ones.

His writing was so vivid that one could almost see the old witch "whose lower lip dangled right down on her chest." It was easy to picture the three dogs with eyes first "as big as saucers," then "as big as millwheels," and finally "as big as the Round Tower of Copenhagen."

When he finished *The Tinder Box,* Andersen began *Little Claus and Big Claus,* another Danish folk tale. A third folk tale followed, *The Princess and the Pea.* This story told of a princess who was so very sensitive that a single pea kept her from sleeping, even though it was underneath a dozen mattresses! Andersen had his friend Henriette Wulff in mind as he wrote this tale. He liked to tease her about being fussy over small things.

Next Andersen wrote an original story, *Little Ida's Flowers*. This tale grew out of a trip to the Botanical Garden with a little friend.

In writing these stories, Andersen included some of his own experiences and dreams. There were references to the theater, which he had loved all his life. Storks and flowers and poetry — things that were dear to him — were mentioned often. So were money and food, which he had often had to do without.

There were kings and princes and princesses, such as he had dreamed of since childhood. There was a shoemaker's son, like little Hans Christian. And there was a student who "told such good stories and could cut such amusing figures out of paper" — Hans Christian Andersen himself.

Andersen wrote and rewrote these stories until they were exactly right. Then he gave them to Edvard to find a publisher. He called them *Fairy Tales Told for Children*. They were published as a 61-page pamphlet in May, 1835. Hans Christian Andersen was 30 years old.

12. The Prince and the Beggar

Andersen's first novel, *The Improvisator*, was published the same spring as his first fairy tales. Several months later Hans Christian Andersen wrote to a friend:

> *"The Improvisator* has won me the esteem of Denmark's best and noblest minds. I do not need to worry, thank Heaven, about keeping myself fed. I can even go as far as to say that I've been able to get some pleasure out of life.... I sit in colorful slippers and

lounging robe with my legs on the sofa, the tile stove hums, the teapot is singing on the table, and the incense smells good. I think of the poor boy in Odense who walked about in wooden shoes, and my heart grows soft, and I bless God in His goodness."

He did not even mention the fairy tales which were to bring him fame! He looked on them as "a mere sleight-of-hand with Fancy's golden apples."

However, Andersen was not the only one who did not recognize the importance of *Fairy Tales Told for Children.*

"It's not writing," one literary critic objected. "It's talking!"

A critic on a Copenhagen newspaper wrote that he had nothing against fairy tales for grownups, but he didn't think they were suitable for children! Children, he said, ought to be offered "books with a higher purpose."

"No one," wrote this critic, "will allege that a

C.A. Jensen's portrait of Andersen shows him as
the kind, sensitive person he really was.

child's proper sense of dignity will be stimulated by reading of a princess who rides off on a dog's back to a soldier who kisses her. . . ." He advised Andersen not to waste his time writing fairy tales!

For once, criticism did not bother Andersen. He was too happy about the success of *The Improvisator* to worry about what people thought of his fairy stories. To his delight, the critics had praised his novel. Better yet, his friends loved it. Admiral Wulff went around telling people it was so interesting he could not put it down! Even the Collins liked it, although they said little in appreciation of his dedication. The novel continued to sell.

The little book of fairy tales sold well too. The author was encouraged to write more. Soon he had three other stories ready for Edvard to have published. *The Traveling Companion* was an old folk tale retold, but the other two were original.

The Naughty Boy was about a poet who was shot by Cupid's arrow. This made him fall in love. Undoubtedly the story grew out of one of

Andersen's unhappy love affairs. Each time he fell in love, the girl married another man. No wonder Andersen wrote in this story, "The good poet lay on the floor and wept, because he really had been shot right through the heart!"

Thumbelina was another original Andersen story. Thumbelina, only an inch high, represented his dear friend, tiny Henriette Wulff. Thumbelina slept in a walnut shell and used a rose petal for a blanket. A wicked toad stole her away from her home, and little Thumbelina went through many adventures and sufferings before she found happiness at last.

At the end of the story, Andersen told about Thumbelina's friend, the swallow. He "flew away again from the warm countries, back to faraway Denmark, where he had a little nest over the window of the man who can tell you fairy tales." Andersen meant that the swallow had told him this story.

The second little book of tales was published just before Christmas in 1835. Shortly afterward, Andersen's second novel, *Otto Thostrup*, came off the press. Within the next three years another novel, *Only a Fiddler*, and three more little books of fairy tales were published.

"Really," said Andersen of the fairy tales, "I should drop these trifles and concentrate on my real work." He did not know yet what his real work was!

Andersen still wanted to be Denmark's greatest playwright. He continued to submit plays to the Royal Theater. Some were produced. A few were successful, but not one could be called a really great play.

Now at last Andersen had enough money. He rented rooms in the Hotel du Nord, close to the Royal Theater and quite near the Collin home. He had his beard shaved by a barber every day. He had his hair curled. He wore high starched collars to hide his long neck, and wide trousers to hide the thinness of his long legs. He had a tall hat and a coat lined with velvet. He looked very elegant indeed.

Andersen had many devoted friends, and they took turns inviting him to dinner. Every Monday he went to the Wulffs. On Tuesdays he dined at the Collins, on Wednesdays at the Orsteds, and so on through the week.

In the Collin house Andersen was the "official candle-snuffer." He was so tall that he could blow out all the candles on the table without leaving his place!

He often had fits of deep discouragement, but he could be a very amusing table companion. He was still wildly talkative. He always had a story to tell of something that had happened recently. He could make the smallest incident sound so funny that the whole family went into gales of laughter.

One winter evening, at the Collin house, Andersen saw his own huge galoshes standing beside the smaller ones of the Collin family.

"Look!" he exclaimed. "My galoshes have had little ones!" How the family laughed! Andersen knew that his friends considered him a most amusing companion.

Yet in spite of their affection, Andersen felt that the Danes did not really appreciate him.

His countrymen could not forget his youthful awkwardness and ignorance and poverty. They found it hard to believe that he was becoming a great writer.

To his Danish friends Andersen was still merely Hans Christian, a good fellow, a loyal friend, and a dear companion. But they felt he was terribly vain. For years friends had been trying to make him overcome his vanity.

"Fight against the terrible adversity of your vanity," Colonel Guldberg had advised him, "the most boundless vanity I have ever seen in a human being."

"Whatever you do, my dear Andersen," Mrs. Wulff had once written, "don't flatter yourself by believing that you'll become . . . a Walter Scott, a Shakespeare, a Goethe, or a Schiller, and never ask again which one of them should be your model. . . ."

On another occasion she had written, "Dear Andersen, wake up and don't dream of becoming immortal, for I'm sure you will only be laughed at."

Once Edvard had urged his friend to "give up this silly writing!"

The Collin family could not bear Andersen's habit of reading his work aloud on every possible occasion. Often Edvard would warn his friend, when the two were starting out together for an evening's visit with friends:

"If you start reading your poems or plays, I shall go home!"

And yet, Andersen would remember that in Germany and Sweden and other foreign countries he was asked to read his poems and tell his stories!

Everywhere he went abroad, Andersen was praised and honored. In one foreign harbor, the Danish flag was run up when it was reported that Andersen was on board the incoming ship.

When Andersen visited the university town of Lund in Sweden, the students came marching in hundreds to greet him and serenade him. They took off their blue caps when he appeared on the steps, and stood bareheaded before him.

"When Europe speaks of the great poet H. C. Andersen," said their spokesman, "do not forget that it was the students of Lund who first gave you the public tribute you deserve."

A great German poet told him, "You justly belong to Germany's favorite authors."

In every country he visited, Andersen was entertained in palaces and castles. Many famous people became his friends. There were royal dukes and princes. There were musicians like

Mendelssohn, Liszt, Robert and Clara Schumann, and Jenny Lind. There were writers like Victor Hugo, Alexander Dumas, the Grimm brothers, and Charles Dickens. There were famous artists, sculptors, and actors. Yes, in every country of Europe except Denmark Andersen was treated like a prince.

When he wrote home about his triumphs abroad, Andersen's Danish friends smiled.

"Andersen is boasting again," they said to each other.

Once when he was returning from a trip abroad, another Dane said in his hearing, "Look! Here comes our world-famous orangutan!"

In Andersen's eyes there was no doubt about it—his own countrymen did not appreciate him. He feared that they never would.

"They spit on me," he said, "when all Europe has honored me. At home I am treated like a beggar."

The thing that hurt the most was that the Collins did not take his honors seriously.

"My Denmark lies in the house of the Collins,"

The Little Mermaid, published in 1837, is still a very popular fairy tale.

he told Edvard once. "I wish to be praised, not for my own pleasure, but so that your father will be pleased. I shall only be happy . . . as a poet when your father can say: 'I am proud of him.'"

When nine of his fairy tales were published as a collection in 1837, Andersen wrote in the preface of the new edition:

"A poet is always a poor man in his own country. Fame is therefore the golden bird he has to catch. Time will tell if I catch it by telling Fairy Tales."

13. "Then One Becomes Famous"

The years passed swiftly. They were crowded with traveling and with writing of all kinds. Every year for almost 40 years, Hans Christian Andersen published a little book of fairy tales. He published a total of 168 stories!

About his way of writing the fairy tales, Andersen said:

> "I look into myself, find the idea for older people — and tell it as if to the children, but remembering that Father

and Mother are listening! ... I have masses of material ... often it seems to me that every fence, every little flower says, 'Just look at me, then you'll know my story!' "

The idea of a story usually came suddenly, "just as a well-known song can come to one." He would tell the entire story to a friend, and then he would write it down. But that was only the beginning. The story grew in his mind and changed and developed. He would write and rewrite it, often five or six times, until he was certain it was the best he could do.

Andersen never stopped writing plays and novels and poetry. He always thought of himself as a poet, although he did not publish many books of poems. Of course he could not have written such beautiful fairy tales if he had not been a poet. Finally he learned that his fame rested on his fairy tales. He accepted the fact that they were his real lifework.

When about 30 of the tales had been published,

Andersen told a friend, "I believe—and I should be happy to be right—that the best thing I can do is to write these tales!"

The Little Mermaid was his own favorite story. It was an original tale of a lovely sea creature who saved the life of a human prince and fell in love with him. She was never able to reach her heart's desire of winning the prince for her husband. But she was so good and kind that she won another kind of reward.

In later years this story became one of Denmark's favorites. A statue of the Little Mermaid was placed in the harbor of Copenhagen. It is still there today, a beloved landmark. The Little Mermaid sits on a rock, looking out to sea. Perhaps she is still longing for her prince!

The Emperor's New Clothes is another popular story. In this tale, Andersen poked fun at people who thought that clothes and appearances were more important than one's thoughts and acts. He was laughing slyly at the people who had laughed at him when he was poor and badly dressed.

The Nightingale was written for the famous singer, Jenny Lind. She was the great love of Andersen's life. In this story he told her how lovely she was, and how much good her marvelous voice did in the world. Like the other women whom Andersen had loved, Jenny Lind married somebody else.

The Nightingale begins: "In China, you know,

Jenny Lind, as painted here by Leon-Noel, married Otto Goldschmidt, a pianist.

the Emperor is Chinese, and all the people are Chinese." As he wrote this story, no doubt Andersen's memory went back to his childhood. In his mind he saw a small boy in wooden shoes down at the Odense River. He heard the boy's high sweet voice singing to the Emperor of China.

Andersen's best-known fairy tale is probably *The Ugly Duckling*. In it he got back at the Collin family for all the fun they had made of him through the years. The ugly duckling was teased and tormented because he did not look like the other ducks. In the end he turned out to be a swan. He was far more beautiful than any of the ducks or other barnyard animals. Everybody who had formerly teased the ugly duckling, and tried to make him over, now had to admire and envy him.

The Ugly Duckling was really the story of Andersen's own life. He was a swan who had been born in a duckyard, but he was not recognized as a swan until many years had passed.

In the story, an old woman rescued the ugly

Among the many Danish artists who have illustrated Andersen's fairy tales, the classic artist is
considered to be Vilhelm Pedersen. This drawing
is from *The Ugly Duckling*.

duckling. She represented Jonas Collin. The cat and the hen represented the Collin children. They could not recognize Andersen's talents because these differed from their own.

"In this house the cat was master and the hen was mistress. They always said, 'We and the world,' for they thought themselves half of the world, and much the better half at that. The duckling thought that there might be more than one way of thinking, but the hen would not hear of it.

'Can you lay eggs?' she asked.

'No.'

'Then be so good as to hold your tongue.'

The cat asked, 'Can you arch your back, purr, or make sparks?'

'No.'

'Then keep your opinion to yourself when sensible people are talking.' "

All through his life, people had tried to make Anderson over. His mother had tried to make a tailor of him. The Collin children had tried to make him sensible and practical like themselves. Teachers had tried to make him an ordinary scholar who used perfect grammar and spelling. Danish critics had tried to make him write in the formal, bookish style of the day. But a swan cannot be made into a duck or a cat or a hen, any more than a duck or a cat or a hen can be made into a swan.

"We must be what we are meant to be," Andersen was saying in *The Ugly Duckling.* "We must follow the path that God has set for us."

At last even Denmark realized that Hans Christian Andersen was a swan. At last his fellow countrymen recognized his greatness. He was given his very own seat at the Royal Theater. He was made Councillor to the King. Moreover, the King and Queen often invited him to dinner, and even for week-long visits.

Hans Christian became as much at home in the castles and palaces of Denmark as he once was in its cheap attic rooms. He wrote many of his stories at the country estates of wealthy friends.

Yes, what he had told his mother before he left Odense had turned out to be true: "First one has to suffer terribly. Then one becomes famous."

Andersen is pictured at the country estate of friends, the Melchiors, who often sent their coachman to fetch him.

14. The Happy Ending

In the fall of 1867, when Andersen was 62, he received a letter from the town council of Odense:

"We herewith have the honor to announce to your Excellency that we have elected you an honorary citizen of your home town. Permit us to invite you to meet us here in Odense on Friday, the sixth of December... upon which day we wish to deliver to you the certificate of citizenship."

When Andersen arrived in the town where he was born, he was welcomed as if he were royalty. The town was gaily decorated. The schools were closed so that children could celebrate his visit. All of Odense turned out to greet her most famous son. The bishop greeted him first.

"I have the honor," said the Bishop, "of escorting you to the Palace."

That evening a great banquet was held in the town hall. Andersen was elegantly dressed in a black suit. Colorful medals and decorations were pinned across his breast. He looked very distinguished.

In his hand he held a telegram of congratulations from the King. But he was tired and nervous, and had a terrible toothache. It had been a very full day with all kinds of ceremonies and speeches.

At the end of the banquet Andersen was called to the window. He gazed out at the town where he had spent his childhood and he thought of his father, his mother, and his grandmother. He remembered the hours he had spent with his puppet theater, and the songs he had sung down by the river.

As he acknowledged the cheers of the crowd in the town square below, Andersen said to himself, "A poor boy, I too walked along those streets." Those were the words Aladdin had said as he stood on his palace balcony after he had become rich and powerful.

As Andersen stood at the window, a torchlight parade began in the town square. The marching

At long last, Odense honored its famous son.

children sang a song he himself had written a few years earlier, "In Denmark I Was Born."

Each verse ended with the words, "'Tis you I love—Denmark, my native land!"

Every time he heard those words, a lump came into Andersen's throat. No matter how far and wide he traveled, there was no place so dear to him, ever, as Denmark. How wonderful it was that his native land had at last recognized his talent!

Down in the square everything glowed brightly. Light shone from lanterns which hung at every door. Light came from a great bonfire in the center of the square, and from the torches of the marchers. All of Odense was lighted in Andersen's honor!

Suddenly Andersen remembered something. It was the prophecy which the old fortune teller had made when he was getting ready to leave Odense: "He will be a wild bird flying high, admired by all the world. One day Odense will be decked with lights for him."

The prophecy had come true! How proud his

mother and father would have been if they could have seen the parade! Andersen's heart was very full as he watched the rest of the ceremonies. When the certificate of citizenship was handed to him, Andersen knew it would be one of his greatest treasures.

Two years later Copenhagen too honored Andersen. The city celebrated the fiftieth anniversary of his arrival there. A fine banquet was attended by 244 important people. The King of Denmark made Andersen a Commander of the Dannebrog. This was a great honor. The university made him a professor. Truly, the ugly duckling had become a swan, and everybody admired him!

He was really a national hero. Even the Collins acknowledged at last that their "queer adopted brother" was a credit to the family.

Andersen lived to see himself recognized throughout the world as Denmark's most famous man. A London newspaper called him "the most-read poet of the age." It said that his fairy tales ranked with Homer and Shakespeare.

Andersen's cup of happiness was full. He had reached his goal. Like his ugly duckling, when he was recognized at last as a swan, Andersen, too,

"... thought about how he had been persecuted and scorned, and now he heard them all call him the most beautiful of all beautiful birds. . . . He rustled his feathers and held his slender neck high, as he cried out with a full heart: "I never dreamed there could be so much happiness, when I was the ugly duckling.""

To the end of his life the theater kept its enchantment for Andersen. He grew too old and feeble at last to attend the theater, but he would follow the play in his mind.

"Now they have reached the quarrel scene," he would say, or, "It is time now for the love scene, I think."

One morning, far too early for the Royal Theater to open, Hans Christian Andersen went

This photograph of Andersen was taken in Germany in 1862 when he was 57.

to sleep forever. The curtain had come down on the play that was Andersen's life. The "beautiful fairy tale" had ended. It was August 4, 1875, and he was 70 years old.

The fairy tale had a happy ending, as fairy tales should. Andersen had truly become rich

137

and famous, even though the fame had come through the fairy tales rather than the theater. In a way, the tales are theater. In them everything is expressed in speech and in action, as on the stage.

The riches too came in a different way than Andersen had expected. He never made a fortune in money, although he had enough to live comfortably. Still, he was very rich in friends all his life.

After Andersen's death Edvard Collin wrote of his friend: "I have looked into the depths of his soul . . . I know *that he was good.*"

How those words would have touched and pleased Hans Christian Andersen!

In the century which has passed since most of Andersen's writing was done, his novels and plays and poetry have been nearly forgotten. Yet the beautiful fairy tales are still known and loved all over the world by children and grownups. The stories are never out of print. Each is as fresh as the day that Hans Christian Andersen wrote it. It seems as if his fame will last forever.

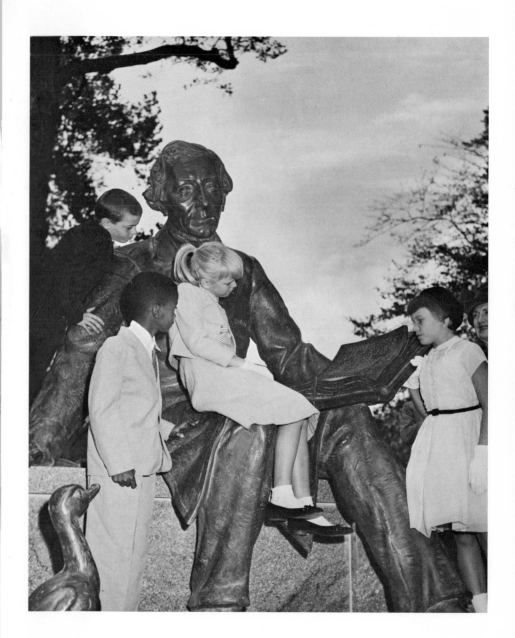

SOME OF ANDERSEN'S BEST-LOVED TALES

Index

Elizabeth Rider Montgomery was born in Peru and spent her childhood in Missouri, where her father, a missionary, had been transferred. She attended college on the West Coast and eventually settled in Seattle, where she now lives.

After college, Mrs. Montgomery became a teacher, a step which led to her later work. She became convinced that she could write a better primer than the ones used by her first graders. She succeeded, and her career was launched.

A versatile author, Mrs. Montgomery has written fiction, nonfiction, textbooks, and plays. Most of her work is for children, and she has had many articles in children's magazines. She is the author of five other Garrard books in addition to *Hans Christian Andersen*.

Richard Lebenson has done most of his illustration work while studying graphics at Pratt Institute, from which he graduated in 1966. He expects to receive a Master of Fine Arts degree from Pratt in June, 1968.

Mr. Lebenson has worked as a portrait artist at the New York World's Fair, has designed greeting cards for a leading card company, and has had his prints on exhibition in New York's Lincoln Center. He has also illustrated a number of children's books.

Born in Queens, New York, in 1946, Mr. Lebenson now lives in Brooklyn. He is unmarried and is a sports enthusiast.

Date Due